Simply Science

FEARLESS FLYERS

Gerry Bailey

Illustrations: Steve Boulter & Xact Studio

Diagrams: Karen Radford

AUTHORS: **GERRY BAILEY**

CONSULTANT: **STEVE WAY**

EDITOR: **FELICIA LAW**

ILLUSTRATORS:

          STEVE BOULTER

          XACT STUDIO

DESIGN: **RALPH PITCHFORD**

          FANNY MASTERS

ISBN 978-1-906292-12-6
Printed in China

PHOTO CREDITS:

p.4-5 Michael Rolands/Shutterstock Inc.
p.6 (c) JoLin/Shutterstock Inc., (b) NASA/GSFC.
p.8 Topfoto.
p.9 (t) Manoir du Clos Lucz/Dagli Orti/The
Art Archive, (b) Mary Evans Picture Library/Alamy.
p.11 Petros Tsonis/Shutterstock Inc.
p.15 (t) Kristian/Shutterstock Inc.,
(br) Tim Zurowski/Shutterstock Inc.
p.17 Karen Hadley/Shutterstock Inc.
p.20 (t) Adrian Steele/Shutterstock Inc.,
(b) Roger Violet/Topfoto.
p.21 Tim Jenner/Shutterstock Inc.
p.23 Foster/The Flight Collection.
p.25 NASA.
p.26 (t) Mark Bond/Shutterstock Inc.,
(c) Richard A. McGuirk/Shutterstock Inc.,
(b) Graham Taylor/Shutterstock Inc.
p.27 (t) Anson Hung/Shutterstock Inc.,
(c) Roger Violet/Topfoto, (b) Topfoto.
p.28 (tr) Chris H. Galbraith/Shutterstock Inc.,
(bl) Popperfoto/Alamy.
p.29 (t) Joel Bauchat Grant/Shutterstock Inc.,
(b) Tomasz Gulla/Shutterstock Inc.

Cover
Arthur Eugene Preston/Shutterstock Inc.

FEARLESS FLYERS

Contents

What is flight?

Flight is movement through the air. It's something birds and some animals can do and something that people have always wanted to do.

Of course, because we don't have wings, we need help. And that's where wonderful inventions such as the hot air balloon, glider and aeroplane come in. They make flying possible for you and me.

So let's go flying:

like a **bird**

like a **hot air balloon**

or a **helicopter**

or even a **jumbo jet**.

Let's soar into space

like a **rocket**.

Balloons are filled with hot air in preparation for flight.

Air that presses

When we jump off the ground, we soon come down again. We can't jump very far at all because something is pressing down on us that stops us. It's the air that stops us.

Probably, when you look up in the air you don't see much – perhaps the odd bird, or cloud or plane. But that doesn't mean there's nothing there!

The 'air' you look at is part of a layer of gases called the 'atmosphere' that wraps around the Earth like a blanket. It helps us keep warm and protects us from harmful rays and too much heat from the Sun. When the air moves we call it wind – so you can actually feel it.

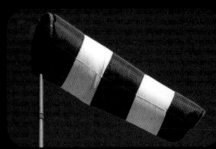

A windsock fills with wind and shows the direction in which it is blowing.

What is air pressure?

The atmosphere is heavy and presses down on us. This pressure is called air pressure. The further up we go in the atmosphere, the less of it there is to press down on us – so the less air pressure there is. Unfortunately, less air means less oxygen to breathe, and humans need oxygen to live!

15% oxygen in air

Molecules

Air is made up of molecules of different gases. Down at sea level, there are lots of oxygen molecules in the air, 21% in fact. But high on the mountain, there are fewer molecules, so less oxygen – only about 15%, and many people find it difficult to breathe easily.

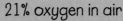

21% oxygen in air

Light things can fly

People used to think that flying was possible if you were lighter than air. They looked at birds' wings and realised that their special shape might help.

They also looked at balloons filled with air that rose easily through the atmosphere.

What was the answer to flying?

Leonardo's flying machines

Leonardo da Vinci lived over 500 years ago in Italy. Most people think he was the cleverest inventor who ever lived.

Leonardo was a genius. He drew pictures of different kinds of machines that no one had ever thought of before and no one actually built until hundreds of years later. These are some of his wonderful flying machines.

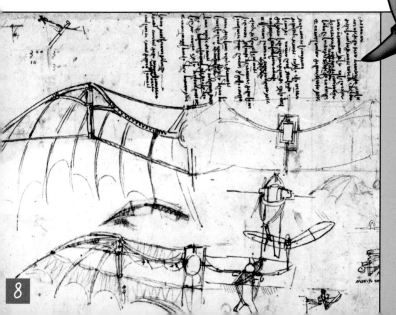

Parachute
Leonardo's parachute used a tent shaped "canopy", or top piece, to catch the air and slow it down as it fell.

Flying machine
Leonardo's flying machine looks like a modern glider.

Helicopter

Leonardo's design for a helicopter used a kind of screw mechanism to lift it off the ground. It looks very modern for the times.

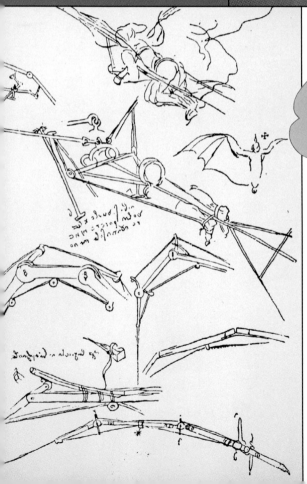

Glider

The glider in this picture has wings that look very much like a bird's wings. Leonardo knew the basic principles of flying, such as lift and aerodynamics.

The Kite

It's great fun flying kites. But do you know how long kites have been around? Scientists believe they were invented in China over 2,000 years ago!

A kite is a kind of aircraft. Usually it's made of something very light, such as cloth or paper that's stretched over a frame. It's flown, or controlled, from the ground by a long cord.

Message on the wind

1. Long ago, armies didn't have technology to help them scout out the size of an advancing enemy. They had to use their eyesight, which meant getting dangerously close.

2. Sometimes they had to send the information they gathered back to camp. But what if the enemy was in the way? They might need to run through enemy ranks.

I don't like the idea of that!

Wind energy

Kites use wind energy to power them. Wind energy can also be used to power sailing boats and wind surfs.

3. They could tape a message to a bird and hope it flew in the right direction...

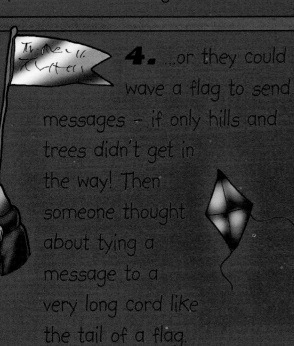

4. ...or they could wave a flag to send messages – if only hills and trees didn't get in the way! Then someone thought about tying a message to a very long cord like the tail of a flag.

5. They made a cross-shaped frame and stretched the cloth over it. The cloth was able to carry a message, while the 'kite' could be controlled from the ground by its long cord.

The hot air balloon

A hot air balloon is a kind of aircraft that uses hot air to make it lift off the ground. The first people to actually fly in the air were carried in the passenger basket of a hot air balloon.

You often see hot air balloons today because of us.

Powered by hot air

1. The Montgolfier brothers loved the idea of flying. They wanted to fly themselves.

2. But they didn't have wings to flap like birds.

3. They noticed, though, that light objects such as leaves floated in the air.

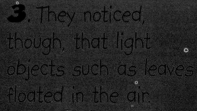

4. They also saw that smoke rose up and floated. They experimented with smoke-filled bags and made the bags rise.

Lifting off

Hot air is lighter than cold air, so it rises through the colder air around it. When a balloon is filled with hot air, the air inside makes the whole balloon rise, as well as the basket underneath that holds the passengers.

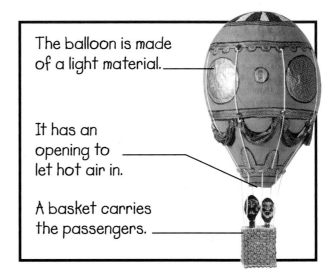

The balloon is made of a light material.

It has an opening to let hot air in.

A basket carries the passengers.

5. Then they found out it was the hot air not the smoke itself that rose. So they filled bags with hot air and watched them take off.

6. Finally they made a huge bag, big enough to hold a basket that could carry passengers. They filled it with hot air from a fire, then put a duck, a sheep and a rooster in the basket. The animals were the first aircraft passengers!

13

Why birds can fly

Wouldn't it be wonderful to fly like a bird? Unfortunately we'd need wings to do that. The special shape of a bird's wings allows it to fly.

Wing shape

A bird's wings are curved in a smooth, streamlined shape. As the wing moves through the air, it divides the air into two flows, one travelling over the wing, and one underneath.

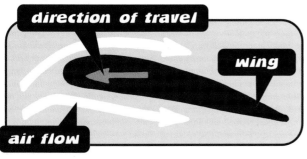

The two flows of air move differently and it is this that helps 'lift' the wing.

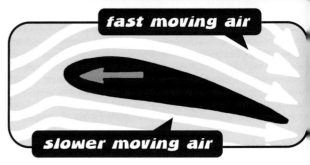

The air moving over the top is bent around the top of the wing. It pulls on the air above, making it move downwards and faster. This faster moving air has lower pressure than slower moving air below the wing. The higher air pressure below the wing also pushes it upwards.

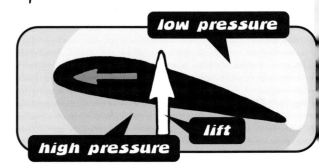

The angle of the wing in the air and combination of air pressure is what gives it lift.

14

The wings of soaring birds, like this eagle, inspired people to design flying machines.

On a plane, the wings act like a huge 'scoop'. As they scoop, or pull air down, the air pressure becomes lower above the wing and helps the plane to rise even more.

A hovering bird

Humming birds can hover by rotating their wings in a very fast figure-of-eight motion. Some species can beat their wings up to 80 times a second!

Flying like a bird

1. The American brothers, Orville and Wilbur Wright made bicycles, but their real love was flight. They knew hot air balloons could fly but they wanted to invent an aircraft that had its own power. They also wanted to control its direction and speed.

2. They knew the wings would be an important part of the machine. These must be shaped like the buzzard's wings they had studied.

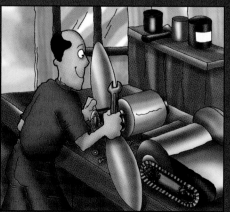

3. They also needed to install an engine to drive the blades of the propeller. The propeller acted as a set of rotating wings and was needed to help the plane rise through the air.

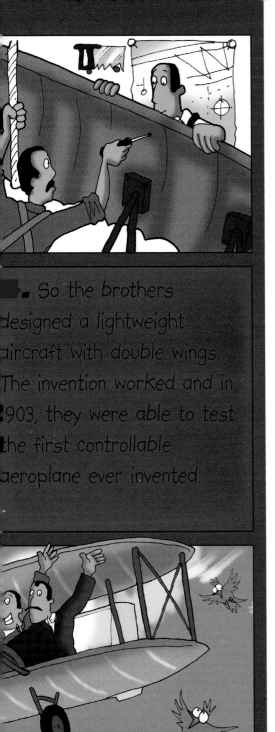

... So the brothers designed a lightweight aircraft with double wings. The invention worked and in 1903, they were able to test the first controllable aeroplane ever invented.

The aeroplane

An aeroplane is a heavier-than-air aircraft that has wings and is powered by an engine.

The American inventors, Orville and Wilbur Wright invented the first aeroplane. They studied buzzards to see how their wings helped them fly and what shapes worked best. They were determined to start a new era of human flight.

Early planes copied the basic lightweight design of the Wrights' first successful plane.

Controlling flight

The Wright brothers, and the inventors who came after them, had to perfect lots of different bits to make controlled flight easy and safe. Here are some of them.

The controls

The Wrights built aeroplanes powered by propeller engines. But they also invented ways to control the craft while it was in the air. 'Elevator' flaps made the nose go up and down and allowed the pilot to dip the aeroplane. A rudder turned it left and right.

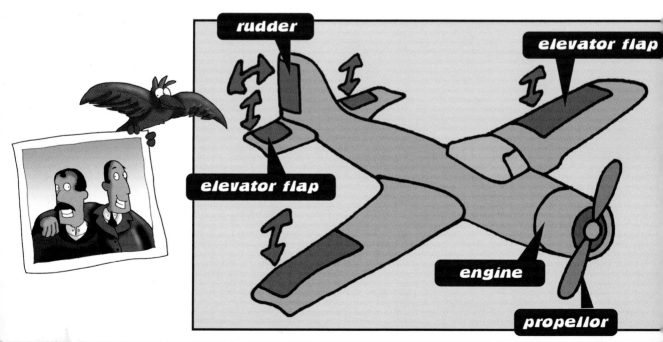

rudder

elevator flap

elevator flap

engine

propellor

Propeller

A propeller acted like moving wings to drive the plane forward. Aircraft, such as the Hurricane, had a propeller in its nose. Engineers had to make sure the guns didn't shoot the propellers off!

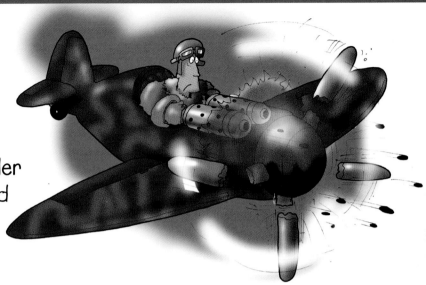

Wheels and pontoons

Landing a plane safely is almost impossible if it has to skid to a stop! So wheels were added to the undercarriage to make the landing safer. Some planes were able to land on water. They had air-filled tanks, called pontoons, fixed below the plane.

Over the years, propeller-driven aircraft became more streamlined and easier to fly. 'Streamlined' means having a smooth shape that causes little friction.

Planes also became faster and safer. The more streamlined a plane is, the faster it will go.

These early planes were called bi-planes because they had two wings. They weren't very fast.

Large planes for carrying goods and passengers needed more power, so they had two or sometimes four engines attached to the wings. The first ones weren't very aerodynamic.

The fighter planes of World War II also had smooth lines. They could manoeuvre much better than earlier planes. They used this ability in dogfights with enemy aircraft.

This Airbus A380 has a smooth aerodynamic shape. It can cruise at very high speed.

So! It's all to do with aerodynamics,

Jet power

The more pilots flew, the faster they wanted to go. Propeller engines were built with bigger engines for more power. But there was another kind of power that aircraft designers knew would make planes faster and even sleeker. It was the jet engine.

A jet engine doesn't need propellers. Instead fuel and oxygen are burned in a compartment in the engine. The burning makes hot gas shoot out of the back of the engine while pushing it forward in the opposite direction.

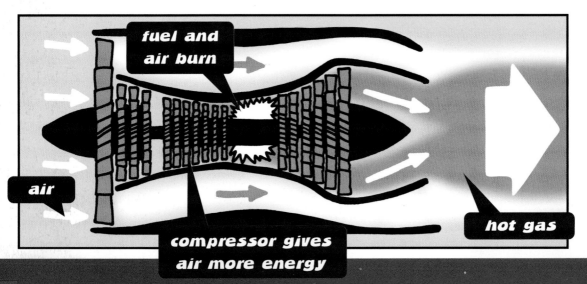

fuel and air burn

air

compressor gives air more energy

hot gas

Planes with jet engines can travel faster than the speed of sound – that's as fast as 1,200 kilometres per hour!

The rocket

When pilots had conquered the air, they started looking beyond it. Perhaps they could journey into outer space. But they'd need something really powerful to do it. They'd need a rocket!

Rocket power

A rocket is a flying machine that's powered by exploding gases. It uses fuel, such as nitrogen, that is mixed with oxygen. The fuel can be in solid or liquid form.

When the fuel and oxygen are mixed and ignited, they expand, or grow larger, very quickly. The expansion creates a huge force or explosion, that pushes the rocket forward. The push is called the rocket's 'thrust'.

1. Scientists wanted to build a craft that would fly to the moon. But it would need huge amounts of fuel to power it away from the Earth.

2. The fuel would explode and create the expanding gas to thrust the rocket upwards.

A controlled explosion

3. In 1926, a scientist called Robert Goddard designed the first liquid-fuel rocket, but it was very small.

4. In 1932 he made a larger cigar-shaped rocket with fins and controls for stability. It didn't go very far though – just 60 metres.

5. Goddard proved rockets could work. And by 1969 rockets had powered astronauts to the Moon and back.

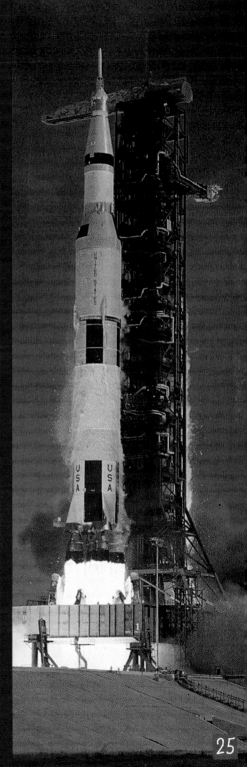

25

Fighter planes

Perhaps the most exciting aircraft to see and hear are the ones used for fighting, They're fast, sleek and make a terrific noise.

Lancaster bomber

Pilots flew Lancasters across Europe to drop bombs on Germany during World War II. The Lancaster had gun turrets where gunners could fire at attacking fighters.

Fokker triplane

The Fokker triplane was flown in World War I. It carried two machine guns and could fly at 200 kilometres per hour.

Hawker Hurricane

The Hurricane was used to shoot down German bombers during the Battle of Britain in 1940. Often mechanics fixed the gun mechanisms so that pilots could fly much closer to their targets than was considered safe.

Sabre

The American jet, the Sabre, was one of the first jet fighters ever built.

B-52 bomber

The B-52 bomber was flown during the Vietnam war, but it's still being used today.

Blackbird

The Lockheed SR-71 Blackbird, set a world speed record of 2,193 kilometres per hour in 1976.

The helicopter

Aeroplanes are great for flying but they need a long runway to land. The Russian inventor, Igor Sikorsky, thought it would be a good idea to invent an aircraft that could take off and land vertically. So he invented the helicopter.

Leonardo da Vinci designed a helicopter long before Sikorsky, but it was never built.

Igor Sikorsky flies his first helicopter.

VTOL

A helicopter is a VTOL craft. VTOL stands for vertical take off and landing. The blades of the craft turn very quickly, making the air above move very quickly and lowering its pressure. In fact, they act just like a wing, making the higher pressure air below push the helicopter up from underneath.

Go-everywhere-machines

Helicopters can fly forwards, backwards and hover in the air. They can get to the places aeroplanes can't reach. Helicopters are used to carry soldiers from place to place, and to protect them from above. They can also rescue people from remote and dangerous places.

Flight Quiz

1. What kind of engine powers a modern jet fighter?

_____

2. What part of the plane makes the nose go up and down?

_____

3. Can a helicopter fly backwards?

_____

4. Which inventor designed a helicopter with a screw for power?

_____

5. What do we call the weight of air that presses down on us?

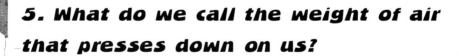

6. What part of a plane makes it lift up into the air?

_____

7. Why can a hot air balloon fly?

_____

8. Who invented the first controllable aeroplane?

_____

9. Which aircraft broke the world air speed record in 1976?

_____

10. What mixture explodes to power a rocket into space?

1. A jet engine 2. An elevator 3. Yes it can 4. Leonardo da Vinci 5. Air pressure 6. The wings 7. Hot air is lighter than cold air 8. The Wright brothers 9. The Blackbird 10. Helium and oxygen

Index